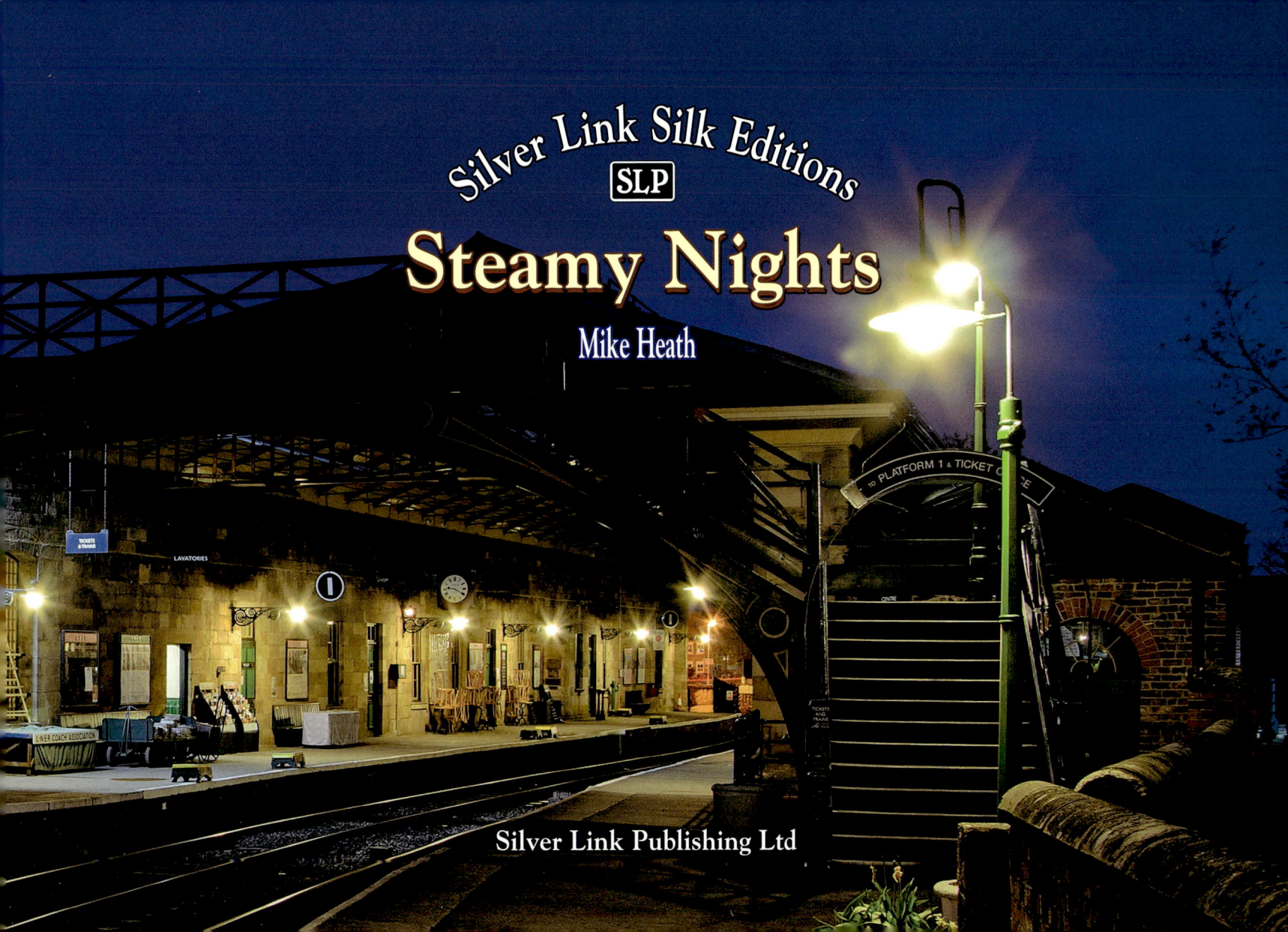

© Mike Heath 2015

All rights reserved. No part of this publication may be reproduced, stored in a retrieval system or transmitted, in any form or by any means, electronic, mechanical, photocopying, recording or otherwise, without prior permission in writing from Silver Link Publishing Ltd.

First published in 2015

British Library Cataloguing in Publication Data

A catalogue record for this book is available from the British Library.

ISBN 978 185794 459 4

Silver Link Publishing Ltd
The Trundle
Ringstead Road
Great Addington
Kettering
Northants NN14 4BW

Tel/Fax: 01536 330588
email: sales@nostalgiacollection.com
Website: www.nostalgiacollection.com

Printed and bound in the Czech Republic

Page 1: Consell signal box on the Churnet Valley Railway. *Karl Heath*

For more information on the preserved railways included in this book their website details are:

Apedale Valley Light Railway – www.avlr.org.uk
Barrow Hill Roundhouse – www.barrowhill.org
Bluebell Railway – www.bluebell-railway.com
Churnet Valley Railway – www.churnet-valley-railway.co.uk
Didcot Railway Centre – www.didcotrailwaycentre.org.uk
East Lancashire Railway – www.eastlancsrailway.org.uk
Embsay & Bolton Abbey Railway – www.embsayboltonabbeyrailway.org.uk
Ffestiniog Railway – www.festrail.co.uk
Foxfield Railway – www.foxfieldrailway.co.uk
Gloucestershire Warwickshire Railway – www.gwsr.com
Great Central Railway – www.gcrailway.co.uk
Keighley & Worth Valley Railway – www.kwvr.co.uk
Kent & East Sussex Railway – www.kesr.co.uk
Llangollen Railway – www.llangollen-railway.co.uk
Midland Railway Centre – www.midlandrailwaycentre.co.uk
NRM Shildon – www.nrm.org.uk
North Norfolk Railway – www.nnrailway.co.uk
North Yorkshire Moors Railway – www.nymr.co.uk
Ribble Steam Railway – www.ribblesteam.org.uk
Rocks by Rail – www.rocks-by-rail.org
Severn Valley Railway – www.svr.co.uk
South Devon Railway – www.southdevonrailway.co.uk
Steamtown, Carnforth – not open to the public
Tanfield Railway – www.tanfield-railway.co.uk
Welshpool & Llanfair Railway – www.wllr.org.uk
West Somerset Railway – www.wsr.org.uk

Title Page (see also page 13): Pickering station is the southern terminus of the North Yorkshire Moors Railway. The overall roof of the original 1845-built station was removed by British Railways in the early 1950s and replaced with platform canopies. However, between 2009 and 2011 a completely new roof was constructed in keeping with the original design, including roof slates obtained from the same Welsh quarry that had supplied the initial construction.

Contents

Introduction	6
The station	8
Waiting for the train	14
The train now arriving	18
The signal box	20
The loco shed	25
Taking on coal	31
Oil and lamps	33
Ready to be turned	36
Fire irons and braziers	38
Out with the fire	39
Railway people	42
Ready to go	51
The train now departing	56
Night mail	59
Themed events	74
Lancashire & Yorkshire Railway	74
London Midland & Scottish Railway	78
Somerset & Dorset Railway	80
East Coast giants	82
Great Western Railway line-ups	86
Breakdown trains and railway cranes	88
Freight operations	92
Colliery railways	106
Quarry railways	114
GWR railmotor and auto-train	116
Locomotive portraits	120
Narrow gauge	130

Introduction

Let us go back to the heyday of the railways… On the edge of most towns stood the Victorian railway station. In the entrance hall was a welcoming fire to warm the hands of travellers queuing to purchase their tickets. Above the fire was the all-important railway clock; not all people had watches in those days. Across the hall the polished door to the Station Master's office was firmly closed. On the wall to one side was the train information board with its chalked messages. Filling the remaining wall space were posters, works of art in their own right, tempting travellers to visit the sun-soaked beaches of the coastal towns just a train ride away.

Follow the 'To the Trains' indicator through the platform gate, showing your ticket to the inspector, and continue on to the platform. Here there are bench seats to rest weary work-worn limbs, vending machines dispensing gum to chew or chocolate to savour, the kiosk where a hot drink and the evening paper can be purchased. On the station's walls are more posters with their artistic portrayals of beauty spots and landmarks accessible for the price of a train ticket. Rust-chipped enamelled signs adorn the platform fencing, extolling the virtues of products such as Bovril, Bisto, Sunlight Soap, Camp Coffee, Wills Tobacco and Woodbine cigarettes – little did they know!

A porter passes by with his steel-wheeled trolley clattering over the stone paving as he meanders his way through the waiting passengers and their baggage. He might pause to acknowledge the relief footplate crew waiting to take charge of the next locomotive to depart. Across on the far platform, more staff are busy loading steel churns full of milk, destined for the next morning's breakfast tables in towns and cities some distance away. Behind them on the platform are wire-caged trolleys full of parcels to be loaded into the vans on the next train due once the milk train has left.

Beyond the station on that far side is the little goods yard where local produce is transferred from road to rail for transportation to markets across the country or to the coastal docks for export.

Alongside the yard are the locomotive sheds where the simmering engines are serviced, watered and coaled in preparation for their next turn.

Just out of town is the local colliery where the hooter has just sounded to announce a shift change. There, powerful little tank engines are huffing and puffing as they trundle back and forth between the mine and its sidings with wagons full of black gold to fuel the nation's power stations and keep the industrial wheels turning.

The sound of a bell heralds a period of activity in the signal box just beyond the platform end. Levers are pulled, buttons are pressed and a large wheel is turned to open the road crossing gates. More levers are released and the signal drops to give a green light for the Night Mail as it speeds through on the fast line with its 'letters for the rich, letters for the poor'.

The gates remain open and the 'Stand well clear of the platform edge' instruction is bellowed out as the steam-hauled 'local' draws to a halt alongside. Those wishing to travel eagerly seek out an empty compartment before boarding, while those parting company at this point make promises to keep in touch! With the relief crew on the footplate, the locomotive builds up pressure and steam swirls around every coach coupling along the train. The guard slams the doors shut as he returns to his compartment at the rear of the train where his green flag awaits. With flag in hand he waits for the signalman to pull yet more levers to give the 'right away'. The signal drops, the green flag is waved and that late-running passenger risks life and limb to jump aboard at the last minute. The locomotive whistles and with an explosion of steam from the cylinders the train slips and slides away from the station.

Now I accept that this is a somewhat rose-tinted view of the past with no reference to the

Introduction

grit, grime and smog that periodically blighted the industrial heartlands and cities across Britain at the time. However, it does serve to illustrate the influence the railways had on all aspects of everyday life, and it is this that the railway preservation movement has successfully sought to retain and recreate for the benefit of future generations.

Most visitors to today's preserved railways simply seek to enjoy a steam-hauled train ride, admire the beautifully restored locomotives and stations, and perhaps take afternoon tea in the railway's cafe. These are the bread-and-butter customers needed to bring in the money that funds the many restoration projects undertaken by the army of volunteers that are the backbone of the preservation movement across the country. Special events see demonstrations of other aspects of railway heritage, such as freight trains.

Many railway photographers tend to concentrate their lenses on the steam locomotive at the front of the train, and there is nothing wrong with this. However, an increasing number of enthusiastic individuals have liaised with specialist preservation groups to recreate many of the scenes from the past referred to above that would be difficult to police on public open days. These 'off-peak' events are open to photographers who pay a fee to attend. While most are held during daylight hours and feature historically accurate, as far as possible, train formations out on the line, some occur after dark and these tend to reflect recreations of some of the more 'routine' railway operations from years gone by.

The majority of the photographs in this book are from my visits, over many years, to such events and, with 21st-century backgrounds hidden in the darkness, they seek to depict timeless scenes that reflect many aspects of life on and around the railways in the Golden Age of Steam.

I hope you enjoy this nostalgic collection.

The station

Locomotives arrive and depart to the hissing of steam. Passengers scurry along the platform. Porters' luggage trolleys clatter over the joints in the stone paving. Carriage doors slam as the guard secures the train. Sights and sounds of the railway station in the age of steam.

The location is Horsted Keynes station on the Bluebell Railway, which dates from 1882. It was built by the London, Brighton & South Coast Railway as part of the Lewes and East Grinstead line, and was originally a junction station with a branch heading off to Haywards Heath. It has been restored to its mid-1920s Southern Railway condition.
Both Karl Heath

The station

The station

Keighley station, on the Keighley & Worth Valley Railway in West Yorkshire, is typical of a junction between a branch line and the national network. The preserved railway operates from Platforms 3 and 4, with Northern Rail occupying 1 and 2. The station retains many original features, including a superb glass canopy with the original toilets and waiting rooms beneath. The booking office on Platform 4 was formally a Findlay's tobacco kiosk at Manchester's Central station (now an exhibition centre), while the ticket collector's hut was originally a telephone box at Wakefield Kirkgate.

By way of contrast, a little further up the Worth Valley line is Oakworth. This typical Midland Railway country halt has retained its original condition with working gas lamps, stone paving, Edwardian posters and neat well-tended gardens. The internal structure is also unaltered completing an old-world atmosphere that Lionel Jeffries could not resist when looking for a location to shoot *The Railway Children* motion picture in the late 1960s.

Hampton Loade station on the Severn Valley Railway is a quintessential former Great Western Railway 'country station' that has changed little over the years. With road access still difficult, the station continues to reflect the country railway as it once was, where long periods of calm and inactivity, with only the station staff milling around, were occasionally broken by brief periods of frantic activity when two trains arrived at the station at virtually the same time!

The station

Pickering station is the southern terminus of the North Yorkshire Moors Railway. The overall roof of the original 1845-built station was removed by British Railways in the early 1950s and replaced with platform canopies. However, between 2009 and 2011 a completely new roof was constructed in keeping with the original design, including roof slates obtained from the same Welsh quarry that had supplied the initial construction.

Waiting for the train

Toddington station on the Gloucester & Warwickshire Railway, which dates from 1904, is on the former 'Honeybourne Line' that linked Stratford-upon-Avon with Cheltenham. This was built as part of the Great Western Railway's high-speed route from the Midlands to the South West of England, which between 1952 and 1962 saw regular express trains such as the 'Cornishman' speed through as it travelled between Wolverhampton and Penzance.

Waiting for the train

A porter waits hoping to earn a tip by carrying passengers' luggage from the train. He already has his platform trolley in place. Meanwhile the Station Master watches over the foot crossing at the end of the platform – health & safety 1950s style! Our porter is resting at Bewdley station on the Severn Valley Railway, a fine example of preservation, with the porter's trolley carrying parcels awaiting collection, bench seats, enamelled advertisements, milk churns, fire buckets, period lighting and even the porter's bike leaning on the fence – no need to lock it in those days! The Station Master is standing amongst the GWR signage at Hampton Loade station.

Steamy Nights

Hampton Loade station buffet kiosk. Every sort of refreshment, hot and cold, would be available to passengers, together with newspapers and magazines for their enjoyment on the long journey…

…or perhaps a long wait for the train's arrival. These passengers are patiently awaiting the next arrival at Ramsbottom station on the East Lancashire Railway.

Waiting for the train

Waiting for a night train across the Fens? This is the platform at Weybourne station on the North Norfolk Railway. *Karl Heath*

Basic station facilities – inside the building the Station Master's office with associated ticket office, and a waiting room with a warm and welcoming fire. On the platform are luggage trolleys and train destination boards. The locations are Oxenhope and Haworth stations on the Keighley & Worth Valley Railway.

The train now arriving

The train arriving at Platform 1 at Bewdley station is the evening local from Bridgnorth, having called at Hampton Loade, Highley and Arley. The train will terminate at the next stop, Kidderminster.

The train now arriving

A busy scene at Keighley on the Keighley & Worth Valley Railway as 4F No 43924 draws to a halt with a passenger working from Oxenhope while 'WD' No 90733 (masquerading as No 90711, a former Leeds-based locomotive) pulls in with a night freight.

The signal box

From the early days of the railway, train movements have been controlled by way of railway signals and block systems to ensure that all trains operate safely. Initially all points and signals were operated locally, with the signalman having to walk between them to set the correct course for each train movement. It did not take long to realise that this control should be centralised into one building, and the signal box was born. This is Bewdley North signal box at the end of Platform 1 at Bewdley station on the Severn Valley Railway.

The signal box

This page and overleaf: Scenes in and around Swanwick Junction signal box at the Midland Railway Centre at Butterley. The history of this box typifies the work associated with railway preservation. It was originally built at Kettering station in 1913 and closed in December 1987. It was then moved to Butterley and placed in its current position over the weekend of 4/5 June 1988, being recommissioned in the spring of 1990.

The signal box

Above: A signalman at work – at Tenterden Town station on the Kent & East Sussex Railway. *Karl Heath*

Left: A signalman at rest – Swanwick Junction signal box, Butterley.

Above: The single-line token is about to be handed to the footplate crew at Williton on the West Somerset Railway. *Karl Heath*

A signalman's duties included checking each train that passed the box and looking for the red tail lamp attached to the last item of rolling stock to establish that the train was complete. On single lines he also ensured that the footplate crew were in possession of the correct token for the next section of track. Each train movement would then be logged, by hand, in the Train Register Book, which was normally

located on a specially designed desk in the box. This example is in the signal box at Consell on the Churnet Valley Railway. *Karl Heath*

The loco shed

Locomotive running sheds tended to be variations of either 'straight road' or 'roundhouse'. The former could be single or multiple track, run-through or single-ended. The Great Western Society at Didcot has preserved this splendid example of a four-track straight shed. It was built in 1932 and each of its four tracks can accommodate three tender engines or six tank engines. 0-6-0 pannier tank No 3738 (left) and 'King' Class 4-6-0 No 6023 *King Edward II* simmer under the watchful eye of the yard man. Note the water crane just in front of the pannier tank.

The loco shed

Left: 1917-built '4300' Class 2-6-0 No 5322 awaits attention in the shed.

Above: These black and white shots from within the shed at Didcot clearly show the roof structure and in particular the long plywood ventilators designed to carry smoke from locomotives in steam out of the shed.

Right: This photograph could have been taken at one of the Southern Region's larger sheds such as Nine Elms or Salisbury back in the 1960s. However, the reality is that it was taken at Grosmont shed on the North Yorkshire Moors Railway in 1994! 'S15' 4-6-0 No 30841 and 'West Country' 4-6-2 No 34027 rest from their labours during the railway's Autumn Gala.

Britain's last surviving working roundhouse is at Barrow Hill, Staveley, near Chesterfield. It is run by the Barrow Hill Engine Shed Society, which rescued it from dereliction in 1991. The roundhouse was originally completed in 1870 and was in continuous use until closure in 1991. It comprises 24 'roads' around the central turntable.

In September 2013 it played host to the new-build LNER Peppercorn Class 'A1' No 60163 *Tornado*. Constructed by the A1 Steam Locomotive Trust in Darlington over a period of 19 years, *Tornado* moved under its own power for the first time in 2008. Since then it has fulfilled the A1 Society's dream of 'hauling specials on the main line and giving joy to thousands of passengers and linesiders'. *Both Karl Heath*

On 6 February 2014 the exhibits included representatives from three of the pre-Grouping companies that would merge into the LNER in 1923. From left to right are Great Central Railway Class 'D11' 4-4-0 No 506 *Butler-Henderson*, which dates from 1919; 1905-built Great Eastern Railway Class 'J17' 0-6-0 No 8217; and Great Northern Railway Class 'C1' 4-4-2 No 251, which emerged from Doncaster Works in 1902.

On occasions the roundhouse hosts photography evenings when the main lights are extinguished and more subdued, atmospheric lighting is employed. *Author/Karl Heath*

The loco shed

Taking on coal

The main activities of a loco shed include locomotive maintenance and running repairs, boiler washouts, watering and coaling.

Towering over many a shed were coaling towers like this one at Steamtown, Carnforth. (This photograph was taken in 1991 when Steamtown was open to the public as a museum.)

Nos 30926 *Repton* (right) and 5428 *Eric Treacy* rest beneath the coaling tower at Grosmont on the North Yorkshire Moors Railway.

Steamy Nights

The Great Western Railway's coaling arrangements are amply demonstrated at Didcot. Loaded wagons are shunted up the slope into the brick-built coaling stage where they are offloaded and the coal shovelled into wheeled tubs. The tubs are then pushed on to a ramp at the front of the stage and tipped into the tender or coal bunker of the locomotive below. Forming the roof of the coaling stage is a water tank that supplies the water cranes seen earlier in front of the shed.

The loco shed

Oil and lamps

There is a never-ending need to keep all the oil reservoirs topped up to maintain lubrication to the pistons, valves and motion. This is the shed at Didcot.

A collection of oilcans and lamps at Llanfair on the Welshpool and Llanfair Railway.

Left: Barrow Hill Roundhouse. *Main photo Karl Heath*

Above: Didcot

Right: Oiling round BR Standard Class 4MT 2-6-4 tank No 80080 at the Buckley Wells shed of the East Lancashire Railway.

Opposite: An 'A4' receives attention at Barrow Hill.

The loco shed

Ready to be turned

In order to ensure that tender locomotives were facing the right way for their next duties, turntables were provided. A locomotive had to be precisely placed over the midpoint to balance the turntable so that it pushed round as easily as possible. However, electric motors were introduced at many locations and some had the facility to connect to the locomotive vacuum brake pipe to turn the table by steam!

This is *King Edward II* on the turntable at Didcot.

The loco shed

The Worth Valley Railway's 4F No 43924 is turned at Keighley station.

Fire irons and braziers

Removing ash from the firebox and cleaning out the remnants of the fire are the biggest and dirtiest of jobs that have to be carried out. Tools of the trade include prickers, darts and clinker shovels, some of which have to be of sufficient length to reach the front of the firebox from the footplate.

The rack in the yard at the East Lancashire Railway's Buckley Wells shed carries an assortment of tools, and on a cold winter's night the brazier helps to keep the staff warm and frost away from the water in the locomotive tenders and pipework.

The loco shed

Out with the fire

The disposal of the fire creates a pyrotechnic display that delights photographers at the end of a night shoot.

Left: No 4936 *Kinlet Hall* at Bridgnorth on the Severn Valley Railway.

Above and right: King Edward II and an 0-4-2T at Didcot.

Above: 0-6-0T *Courageous* at the Ribble Steam Railway, Preston.

Right and far right: The Webb 0-6-2 'Coal Tank' and well tank *Bellerophon* at Haworth on the Keighley & Worth Valley Railway.

The loco shed

Railway people

A pause for conversation at the Didcot Railway Centre.

Opposite: On a cold and wet night at Barrow Hill there are still duties to perform.

Railway people

'Climbing aboard' on shed at Buckley Wells on the East Lancashire Railway.

Railway people

Footplate crews rest their weary limbs at Hampton Loade on the Severn Valley Railway…

…and at Tenterden on the Kent & East Sussex Railway.
Karl Heath

Railway people

Railway people

'Awaiting the off' at Swanwick Junction station (Midland Railway Centre), Bolton Street station (East Lancashire Railway) and Keighley station (Keighley & Worth Valley Railway).

Left: Pause for thought by Swanwick Junction signal box, Midland Railway Centre.

Right: Staverton station on the South Devon Railway.

Ready to go

Getting 'ready for the off' at Tenterden station on the Kent & East Sussex Railway. The locomotive is a former London, Brighton & South Coast Railway 'A1X' Class 0-6-0 tank, a class known to enthusiasts as 'Terriers'. Currently in its British Railway guise as No 32670, it emerged from Brighton Works in 1872. One of ten surviving members of the class, No 32670 has a long-standing association with the line, having spent much of its working life on the K&ESR. The distinctive coach dates from 1910 and is a South Eastern & Chatham Railway 'Birdcage' Brake, so-called because of the raised guard's look-out at the end. *Karl Heath*

At Ramsbottom on the East Lancashire Railway, British Railways Standard Class 4MT 2-6-4T No 80080 is just waiting for the crossing gates to open to allow it to continue its journey to Rawtenstall.

Ready to go

At the North Norfolk Railway's Weybourne station, BR Standard Class 4MT 2-6-0 No 76084 is raring to go onwards to the railway's terminus at Holt. *Karl Heath*

Ready to go

Left: 'Chomping at the bit' at Hampton Loade station, Severn Valley Railway, is Great Western Railway 'Hall' Class No 4936 *Kinlet Hall* with steam to spare as it patiently waits for the green light.

Right: A brace of 'Bulleids' are about to take the strain at Toddington. As part of its 2015 Cotswold Festival of Steam, the Gloucestershire Warwickshire Railway arranged for two Southern Region 'Pacifics' that had both once been based at Salisbury shed to be reunited for a couple of weekends. No 34007 *Wadebridge* was visiting from the Mid-Hants Railway, while No 34092 *Wells* had ventured south from the Keighley & Worth Valley Railway. On 30th May an evening charter concluded with a night shoot at the station.

The train now departing

The wait is over for 'A1' *Tornado* as the signal drops at Hampton Loade.

Opposite: A powerful double departure from Loughborough station on the Great Central Railway stars 'Black 5s' Nos 45305 and 45231 *The Sherwood Forester*.

The train now departing

Southern Railway Class 'E4' 0-6-0T No 473, built in 1898, eases past the splendid array of signals that control all movements out of Horsted Keynes station on the Bluebell Railway. *Karl Heath*

Night mail

This page and overleaf: In the early days of rail, mail was carried by normal passenger trains, while rural deliveries utilised horse-drawn GPO postal delivery carts. It was not long before a mail sorting coach in the form of a converted horse box had been developed to allow mail to be sorted on the move. From this developed designated mail trains known as Railway Post Offices up to 1928 and Travelling Post Offices (TPOs) from then on.

In October 2001 the Severn Valley Railway-based Friends of the Locomotive 'Hagley Hall' Preservation Society organised a 'Mail Train' photo-charter that ended with a night shoot at Bewdley station. I cannot look at these photographs without hearing the words, and the rhythm of John Betjeman's rendition of W. H. Auden's famous poem 'Night Mail'!

The locomotive in the starring role was 'Black Five' 4-6-0 No 45110 *RAF Biggin Hill*, which was built for the London Midland & Scottish Railway at the Vulcan Foundry in Newton-le-Willows in 1935. This locomotive has its own place in railway history, being one of those in sufficiently good condition to take part in the official British Railway's 'Farewell to Steam' rail tour in August 1968.

Night mail

The transport of railway parcels was a special high-value category of sundries traffic. Parcels were carried in the guard's compartment of passenger trains or in special trains of parcel vans. A classic feature of these operations was the four-wheeled trolley used to move the mail bags and parcels across the platforms. British Railways specifically developed these wire-caged trolleys with a low floor to replace the existing platform luggage trucks. These scenes taken at Bolton Street station, East Lancashire Railway.

Based on the East Lancashire Railway, the 3P20 Parcels Group is a non-profit-making volunteer-run organisation dedicated to the preservation of parcel-carrying stock used by British Railways. (The 'name' 3P20 was the reporting number for one of the last regular steam-hauled parcel trains operated by British Railways in 1968.)

In addition to the restoration of appropriate rolling stock, the group holds 'themed' photographic events to both raise funds and make use of its ever-increasing collection of restored vehicles. One such event was held at the ELR's Bolton Street station in February 2011. At the head of the parcels train was the Severn Valley Railway's 2MT 2-6-0 No 46443, while standing across the platform with the next passenger train departure was the Midland Railway Centre's 5MT 4-6-0 No 73129. Suitably attired station staff and passengers completed this 1950s cameo, to say nothing of the plethora of parcels strewn across the platform. On this occasion the guard appears overawed by the apparent single-handed task before him.

Night mail

Night mail

That evening also stirred memories of the unforgettable 1946 motion picture *Brief Encounter*, where two strangers meet on a railway station and their casual acquaintance develops into something more emotional!

Pages 68-72: However, back to parcels trains! March 2013 saw a 'parcels' scenario set up at Ramsbottom station, where a Royal Mail van provided added interest.

Night mail

One year later, in March 2014, the Midland Railway Centre at Butterley hosted a similar event. The driver and fireman have a well-earned brew as they watch parcels being loaded prior to departure.

Night mail

This particular event was a collaboration between the organisers of 30742 Charters and 'Lure of Steam Photographic Events', which meant that a number of scenes could be lit up at the same time, giving multiple photography angles.

Themed events

Lancashire & Yorkshire Railway

This title was given to the railway company that emerged following the absorption of a number of local railways by the then Manchester & Leeds Railway in 1847. It served the industrial heart of the North West of England and linked this with the mineral wealth of Yorkshire, developing a large and complex railway system with shipping interests on both the north-west and north-east coasts. The large ceramic map that adorns a wall inside the Hunts Bank entrance to Manchester Victoria station, dating from around 1904, clearly illustrates the routes of the L&YR system. In 1923 the company became part of the London Midland & Scottish Railway company.

Left: The Lancashire & Yorkshire Railway Trust, based on the Keighley & Worth Valley Railway in West Yorkshire, owns a unique collection of steam locomotives and carriages previously owned by that railway. In October 2012 the KWVR held a gala at which one of the trusts's working locomotives was paired with another privately owned example at the head of a trio of restored carriages.

Visiting L&YR Class '27' 0-6-0 No 1300 (nearest the camera) was built in 1896 at the railway's Horwich Works, while the Trust's L&YR Class '25' 0-6-0 No 957 emerged from the Beyer Peacock factory in Manchester in 1887. The pair were photographed preparing for an early-evening departure from Keighley station. *Karl Heath*

By the time the train had arrived at the railway's Oxenhope terminus, No 957 had been taken off at Haworth shed. Immediately behind No 1300 is the beautifully restored L&YR Club Carriage that dates from 1912 and had been built for the exclusive use of businessmen commuting between Blackpool and Manchester. Behind that is a six-wheel five-compartment 3rd Class carriage that left Newton Heath works in 1882.

Themed events

This was the overnight scene in the shed yard at Haworth where the pair were lined up alongside a third L&YR locomotive – in the shadows is the diminutive 0-4-0 saddle tank No 51218, another Horwich-built locomotive, this time in 1901.

London Midland & Scottish Railway

The 1921 Railways Act saw the amalgamation of the then independent railway companies into just four, the Great Western, Southern, London & North Eastern, and London Midland & Scottish. The LMS brought together the London & North Western and Midland companies, and several Scottish railways.

At the end of 2014 the East Lancashire Railway at Bury found itself with three representatives from the LMS on its line and therefore put together a mini gala to celebrate. Included as part of the event was an evening photo shoot at the railway's Buckley Wells depot, where the three locomotives posed in a recreation of a 1930s steam shed scene. They were No 13065, a 2-6-0 'Crab' locomotive built in 1927; No 12322, an 0-6-0 'A' Class locomotive built in 1896 (re-liveried as L&YR No 1300); and No 16407, an 0-6-0T 'Jinty' locomotive built in 1926.

Somerset & Dorset Railway

The 'S&D', as it was almost always referred to, was a railway that connected Bath in north-east Somerset with Bournemouth in the south. Colloquially known as 'the Slow and Dirty', it always commanded a considerable loyalty from railway enthusiasts and was much mourned on its closure in 1966.

For its 2002 Spring Gala the Severn Valley Railway held a Somerset & Dorset weekend with the appropriate classes of locomotives renumbered as former S&D locos. Visiting British Railways 4-6-0 No 75014 was numbered 75009, 'Black 5' No 45110 became 45440, and British Railways 2-6-4T No 80079 carried 80043. On the Saturday evening the trio were posed around the water tower at Bewdley station.

East Coast giants

2013 saw the 75th anniversary of the world speed record for steam locomotives set by London & North Eastern Railway Class 'A4' 4-6-2 No 4468 *Mallard* when it reached 126mph on 3 July 1938 at Stoke Bank near Grantham. To celebrate this anniversary the National Railway Museum brought together the only survivors of the 35-strong class of locomotive at a number of events around the country. This involved the temporary repatriation of two of the locomotives from museums across the water. Nos 60008 *Dwight D. Eisenhower* and 4498 *Dominion of Canada* were released for the event by the National Railroad Museum in Green Bay, Wisconsin, and Exporail, the Canadian National Railway Museum in Montreal.

On 20 October 2012, shortly after their arrival back on these shores and in 'as delivered' condition, Nos 60008 and 4498 (60010) posed alongside operational No 60009 *Union of South Africa* at the National Railway Museum, Shildon. The two then underwent cosmetic restoration to their original state in readiness for the main anniversary events at the National Railway Museum, York. *Both Karl Heath*

Steamy Nights

Themed events

In February 2014, following the main celebrations and just before the two 'visitors' headed home, they were taken to Barrow Hill Roundhouse where, on a very wet evening, photographers gathered to get their last shots of Nos 60008 and 4498, this time alongside another fully restored member of the class, No 4464 *Bittern*. Of note is the cosmetic restoration of No 4489 into full 'Coronation' condition complete with chrome trimmings. This was the livery created for the 'Coronation' service operated by the London & North Eastern Railway between London King's Cross and Edinburgh Waverley stations. Named to mark the coronation of King George VI and Queen Elizabeth, the service first ran in July 1937.

Great Western Railway line-ups

The Didcot Railway Centre near Oxford is home to the Great Western Society and its considerable collection of locomotives. Night photography evenings are a regular feature of its events programme, with line-ups such as these being an integral feature.

Above: The first picture from 1997 shows, from left to right, Nos 3738, 4073 *Caerphilly Castle*, 5051 *Earl Bathurst*, 6697 and 5900 *Hinderton Hall*.

Left: The second, from 2002, includes Nos 5900 *Hinderton Hall*, 5051 *Earl Bathurst*, 3822 and 6998 *Burton Agnes Hall*.

Themed events

C. B. Collett designed the 'Manor' Class of locomotives for work on the lighter-constructed Great Western Railway main lines such as the former Cambrian network in mid-Wales. To celebrate the 150th anniversary of the railways in mid-Wales, which were to become an integral part of the Cambrian Railways company, the West Somerset Railway gave a distinct 'Cambrian' theme to its October 2013 Gala. For the first time in preservation four 'Manors' were steamed together, and my son Karl was on hand to record the overnight scene at Minehead station. From left to right are No 7822 *Foxcote Manor* (from the Llangollen Railway), No 7827 *Lydham Manor* (a resident on the Dartmouth Steam Railway), West Somerset-based No 7828 *Odney Manor* and, from the Severn Valley Railway, No 7812 *Erlestoke Manor*. *Karl Heath*

Breakdown cranes and railway cranes

Breakdown cranes and railway cranes

Left: These were once a common sight on British Railways, be it for track maintenance, the re-railing of locomotives, the lifting of boilers or any other heavy-duty lifting requirements. Most preserved railways include a crane in their stock list, many in operational condition. This is the East Lancashire Railway's Cowans, Sheldon 75T crane, which dates from 1960.

Right: This 1939-built Ransome & Rapier 45T steam crane, RS 1097/45, is at Loughborough on the Great Central Railway.

Right: A Cowans, Sheldon RS1054 50T crane stands on the demonstration line at Didcot. This example was built in 1930.

Right: A Thomas Smith & Sons 5-tonne shunting crane takes part in a track maintenance demonstration at Didcot.

Far right: This 0-4-0 crane tank was built by Dübs & Company of Glasgow in 1901. Unofficially named 'Dubsy', it can often be seen demonstrating its lifting capabilities at the preserved mine on the Foxfield Railway.

Breakdown cranes and railway cranes

Freight operations

Right up to the 1950s just about everything was moved by rail. The business of transporting goods around the country consisted of a network of railway goods yards and privately owned sidings, where goods were loaded and/or unloaded, and railway marshalling yards, where individual wagons were sorted into rakes for onward transit to their respective destinations nationwide.

Freight operations

In January 2012 the 3P20 Parcels Group took the opportunity to place the National Railway Museum's 'Super 'D'' locomotive at the head of a freight train in the sidings alongside the East Lancashire Railway's loco sheds, thus recreating a typical yard scene from the early 1950s. Suitably attired volunteers fulfilled the roles of loco driver, guard and yard foreman.

The impressive 0-8-0 goods loco No 49395 was built for the London & North Western Railway in 1921 and worked until retirement, from Buxton, in the late 1950s.

The 'WD' 'Austerity' 2-8-0s were developed in the 1940s as the then new standard heavy freight engine to aid the war effort. They were designed in such a way that any one of several locomotive manufacturers would be able to build them with materials readily available in wartime. The Keighley & Worth Valley Railway's example was built in 1945 and spent its entire working life overseas, firstly in the Netherlands, then for the Swedish State Railway. It returned to these shores in the early 1970s. More than 700 examples of this class were in use on the British Railways network after the war and every one of them was scrapped!

This locomotive is therefore unique and has been restored to the original British outline and given the number 90733, which would have been the next available in the British Railways stock list had it returned from overseas after the war.

For an evening photo charter at Keighley station in March 2014 the smokebox number was changed to 90711, which was the number of a former 'WD' locomotive that had operated locally out of Low Moor shed in Bradford.

Freight operations

Back in 2008, when the locomotive visited the East Lancashire Railway in Bury, it took part in a similar event at Bolton Street station. Unfortunately very few urban stations have been preserved, but those that have, such as Keighley and Bury, do still maintain that railway 'feel' about them.

Based on the Severn Valley Railway, the 2857 Society's 'raison d'être' is the long-term preservation of Great Western Railway heavy goods locomotive No 2857. Built in 1918 and withdrawn from active service in 1963, it was eventually purchased from the famous Barry scrapyard in 1974. When this photograph was taken, at Bridgnorth in September 2011, the loco had just emerged from its fourth overhaul in preservation – the society's aims being well and truly maintained.

Freight operations

The Great Western Railway '2251' Class 0-6-0 tender locomotives were designed by C. B. Collett for medium freight and passenger services. 'Collett Goods' No 3205 emerged from Swindon in 1946 and is the only surviving member of the class. Initially preserved on the Severn Valley Railway, but now based at the South Devon Railway in Buckfastleigh, it returned to the Midlands line as a visitor in September 2012 for its Steam Gala and hauled the overnight freight. It was photographed at Bridgnorth station just prior to departure.

Freight operations

Left: In 2013, as part of a year-long UK tour, the Talyllyn Railway's narrow-gauge locomotive No 3 *Sir Haydn* visited a number of standard-gauge railways. At that year's Severn Valley Railway Gala it was loaded onto a standard-gauge flat wagon and hauled up and down the line. It was photographed while pausing at Bewdley station.

Right: A few weeks later, on 4 October, the diminutive locomotive took part in the West Somerset Railway's Autumn Gala, which had a Cambrian Railways theme. This was most appropriate, as *Sir Haydn* spent all its working life in the Cambrian area, having been built for the Corris Railway. These unusual freight workings re-enacted an old Cambrian tradition of narrow-gauge locomotives being taken by standard-gauge train to the locomotive works for repair. The location of this photograph is Williton station. *Karl Heath*

The Ribble Steam Railway operates on the last surviving part of the former Preston Docks system, and when Bagnall 0-6-0ST No 2680 returned to steam in 2014 it was turned out in the guise of one of the six lost Preston 'Bagnalls'. It emerged from the workshops bearing a pair of newly cast *Courageous* nameplates, together with a pair of tank-side ladders identical to those fitted to its namesake. Soon to follow was the chimney-top 'halo'-type spark arrestor. On 15 February 2014 it is seen shunting appropriate freight wagons in the railway's Riverside sidings.

Freight operations

It must be remembered that right up to the 1950s the railways carried just about everything from raw materials to finished products including farm produce – fresh milk, butter, meat and, of course, livestock. Breweries also used rail transport, and in another unique event, held in February 2012, the 3P20 Parcels Group used the former Castlecroft goods yard to recreate a typical scene from yesteryear. The cameo featured Peckett 0-4-0ST *May* and a brewery dray wagon dating from 1947.

Freight operations

Left: Railways carried milk from as early as the 1930s, and the early-morning 'milk train' was a feature of British life until the late 1960s. The South Devon Railway, based at Buckfastleigh, regularly runs demonstration 'milk trains' during special event weekends. One evening in February 2015 visiting GWR 'Prairie' locomotive No 4566, from the Severn Valley Railway, was placed in charge of the train and was posed at Staverton station, which has remained an unspoilt country station for more than 100 years since it was opened by the Buckfastleigh, Totnes & South Devon Railway in 1872.

Above left and above: While the late 1920s saw the introduction of 3,000-gallon tankers that had been developed to supply greater quantities of milk to the larger towns, milk churns remained a part of the scene well into the 1960s and would be loaded into vans from the station platform.

Colliery railways

The pace of the Industrial Revolution was driven by the ability to transport coal from the mines to industry. Prior to 1750 the roads in Britain were very poor and the movement of goods in bulk was extremely difficult. While ships could transport coal from port to port, this had its own limitations and the natural flows of rivers meant that many were of little use. The initial improvement in transport came with the introduction of canals. In 1761 the Duke of Bridgewater opened a canal from Worsley to Manchester for the express purpose of carrying coal. This initiative brought him wealth and fame as he could increase production to meet the demand for this cheaper coal. Other coal mine owners followed suit. However, the canals were still slow and getting coal to them also had its problems. It was the introduction of steam locomotion in the 1800s that finally brought about a faster and cheaper transport system. As the railways spread, coal mining was stimulated by the increase in coal-fired industries across the country.

It was not long before the coalfields developed their own private railway networks to get their coal from the pithead to the national railway network via transfer sidings and the like. The subsequent destruction of the industry took with it most of the railway infrastructure, but remnants still exist and, as ever, preservationists have stepped in to ensure that all is not lost.

The Foxfield Railway is based on a line built in 1893 to move coal from Foxfield Colliery, in the Cheadle coalfield, to the North Staffordshire Railway at Blythe Bridge. The pithead structures are an excellent backdrop for photography and a number of events have been held there over the years. On 29 December 2013 Hunslet 0-6-0 saddle tank No 3839 *Wimblebury*, built in 1956, took centre stage during another 3P20 Parcels Group charter. This locomotive had spent all its working life locally, at Cannock Wood Colliery in Staffordshire.

Colliery railways

Left: Collieries also had their own sheds and workshops to store and maintain their locomotives, and the Tanfield Railway, in County Durham, the oldest railway in the world, has preserved the Marley Hill engine shed, which dates from 1854.

Two examples of the Class 'Y7' 0-4-0 tanks were photographed outside the shed on 7 September 2012. No 985, built in Darlington in 1923, stands alongside No 1310, a visitor from the Middleton Railway in Leeds, and much older, dating from 1891. *Both Karl Heath*

Right: That same evening, 0-6-0T *Twizell*, built by Robert Stephenson & Company in 1891, was paired with *Renishaw Ironworks No 6*, which emerged from the Hudswell Clarke works in Leeds in 1919. *Karl Heath*

Colliery railways

Left: Out of service inside the shed was the 1943-built NCB 0-6-0 saddle tank No 49. *Karl Heath*

Right: The vintage workshop, forge and wheel lathe in the shed are still capable of full locomotive overhauls. *Karl Heath*

Colliery railways

Another development at Foxfield has been the introduction of the 'Knotty Heritage Train' featuring coaches that date back to the mid-1870s, having been constructed at the North Staffordshire Railway's own works in Stoke-on-Trent. (The term 'Knotty' is derived from the Stafford Knot that appeared in the NSR's coat of arms.) The restoration of these coaches to as close to original condition as possible has been carried out by the North Staffordshire Rolling Stock Restoration Trust.

A handful of these coaches lasted until 1923 in workmen's trains, and it was one such train that was recreated in the colliery sidings on a very wintry December night in 2014. A most appropriate locomotive at the head of the train was the 0-6-0 well tank *Bellerophon*, which was built for the Haydock Collieries in 1874. Society members suitably attired and carrying Davy lamps complete the scene.

Quarry railways

The Rutland Railway Museum, now known as 'Rocks by Rails', is located near Oakham in the ancient county of Rutland and is dedicated to telling the story of railways in industry with particular emphasis on local ironstone quarrying.

Back in 1997 the centre invited photographers for an evening of photography with a number of locomotives and locations illuminated for the purpose. The locomotives on display were Andrew Barclay 0-6-0ST *Salmon*, built in 1942; Avonside 0-4-0ST *Dora*, built in 1927; and vertical-boilered Sentinel 4wVBT No 9376, of 1947.

Quarry railways

The locomotives were also posed in front of the old shed, itself a historic survivor from a local quarry railway.

GWR railmotor and auto-train

At the beginning of the 20th century most railways were looking for a simple train for lightly used services on branch lines, or local trains on the main line in urban areas. Thus the concept of the steam railmotor was developed. The idea dated back to the mid-19th century, but its heyday, for the Great Western Railway in particular, came with the construction of a fleet of 99 steam railmotors between 1904 and 1908. One of their main benefits over traditional steam-hauled coaches was that reversal was easy, without the need for a locomotive to 'run round' its train.

No 93 was built in 1908, converted to an auto-coach in 1934 and withdrawn from service in 1956. It was acquired by the Didcot Railway Centre in 1970 and its rebuilding as a railmotor began between 2007 and 2009 and was completed at Llangollen in 2011. After a period of running in on the Welsh line, it took part in a photo charter that included a night shoot at Llangollen station.

GWR railmotor and auto-train

Two years later, in July 2013, it was working overnight services into Didcot Halt back at its home base of Didcot Railway Centre. This cameo depicts the guard possibly consulting the rule book with the crew offering their own advice!

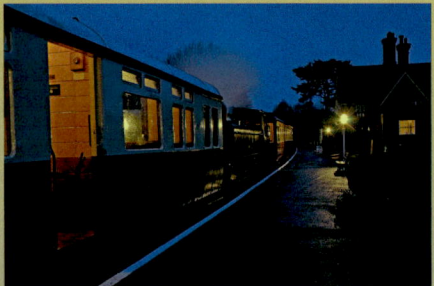

While the steam railmotors in operation were initially successful, their maintenance proved to be problematic. Because of their design, the whole unit had to enter the works for maintenance and repair and this created great difficulty in keeping the passenger accommodation clean. Their boilers were also difficult to remove and maintain.

Thus the 'auto-train' was introduced, where the steam locomotive could be controlled remotely from a 'driving cabin' at the end of the train. From here the driver could operate the regulator, brake and warning whistle, while the fireman remained on the footplate. Steam locomotives provided with the equipment allowing their use in auto-trains were said to be 'auto-fitted' or 'push-pull fitted'.

A number of preserved steam locomotives are 'auto-fitted', including GWR 0-6-0 pannier tank No 6430 on the Llangollen Railway, where auto-train services are operated during special events. These views date from April 2008 and show the auto-train just prior to departure from Carrog *(above and also see front cover)* with an evening service to Llangollen, and a little later *(right)* pausing at a flood-lit Berwyn station en route.

GWR railmotor and auto-train

The South Devon Railway also operates auto-trains utilising its own GWR pannier tank No 6412. During the preserved line's 'Branch Line Week' in February 2015 the auto-train was employed on some evening services and is seen here standing at the timeless Buckfastleigh station. *Karl Heath*

Locomotive portraits

Probably the most historically significant locomotive in the world is the London & North Eastern Railway Class 'A4' No 4468 *Mallard*. As many will know, this locomotive is the holder of the world speed record for a steam locomotive, having achieved 125.88mph travelling down Stoke Bank, just south of Grantham, on the East Coast Main Line on 3 July 1938. As part of the celebrations held to celebrate the 75th anniversary of the event, the locomotive took part in a number of events around the country including a period at the Barrow Hill Roundhouse near Chesterfield. *Karl Heath*

Locomotive portraits

Arguably the most famous steam locomotive is LNER Class 'A3' No 4472 *Flying Scotsman*, which was built at Doncaster in 1923 and went on to a career as the LNER's flagship locomotive, beginning when it was selected to appear at the British Empire Exhibition in 1924. In 1928 it was given a new type of tender with a corridor allowing a new crew to take over on the footplate without stopping the train. On 1 May of that year it hauled the first ever non-stop London to Edinburgh service. Six years later, in 1934, it clocked 100mph, becoming officially the first locomotive to have reached that speed.

In 1993 it visited the East Lancashire Railway and was photographed on a very wet evening at Ramsbottom station. It is currently undergoing overhaul and is expected to be returned to active service in late 2015/early 2016.

Right: Other locomotives achieving fame, albeit in just railway folklore, did so by surviving the demise of steam to take part in the last steam-hauled passenger train on British Railways. That honour fell to BR Standard 'Britannia' Class 7 No 70013 *Oliver Cromwell*, which unsurprisingly was the last British Railways-owned steam locomotive to undergo a routine heavy overhaul, being outshopped in 1967. In February 2010 it visited the East Lancashire Railway for its Winter Gala and was posed outside Buckley Wells shed.

Below right: That last steam-hauled rail tour, on 11 August 1968 – 'The Fifteen Guinea Special' – ran from Liverpool to Carlisle and back, and No 70013 hauled the Manchester to Carlisle leg. The return leg, Carlisle to Manchester Victoria, was double-headed by 'Black 5s' Nos 44871 and 44781. No 44871 has also been preserved and is based at Bury, so the opportunity to reunite these locomotives was too good to miss. To complete the occasion, the 1T57 reporting number carried by that last train was placed on the 'Black 5'.

* Publisher's note: The Liverpool to Manchester Victoria section on the outward journey and the Manchester Victoria to Liverpool section on the return journey were both hauled by a single 'Black 5' No 45110. This locomotive also survives, preserved on the Severn Valley Railway, and is now named *RAF Biggin Hill*.

Locomotive portraits

Right: The National Railway Museum's LNER Class 'V2' 2-6-2 No 4771 *Green Arrow* was the first built of the class, and is the only surviving member. It emerged from Doncaster Works in June 1936, having been specifically designed for hauling express freight and passenger trains. It was withdrawn in 1962, and became part of the National Collection. Having spent many years hauling services on both the main line and at preserved railways, the locomotive was finally stopped in April 2008 and is now back at the NRM in York with, unfortunately, little hope of further restoration to working order. This photograph was taken in its final year of operation, at the Churnet Valley Railway, Cheddleton.

Below: Another 'first of class' to be preserved was the Southern Railway's 'Lord Nelson' Class 4-6-0 No 850 *Lord Nelson*, which dates from 1926, having been built at the SR's Eastleigh Works.

Overleaf: GWR 'King' Class No 6023 *King Edward II* is one of only three surviving members of this heavy express locomotive class. It was built in June 1930, withdrawn in 1962 to spend many years in the scrapyard at Barry Island. Even though it was saved in 1974, it had to remain in the yard for several more years as its rear driving wheels had been flame-cut following a derailment, making further movement extremely difficult. However, in 1985, as part of the 150th anniversary of the Great Western Railway's formation, the rusting hulk was taken over by Harvey's of Bristol and moved to a bay platform at Bristol Temple Meads station. It was later bought by the Great Western Society and moved to Didcot in March 1990. Restoration over many years saw it move for the first time in preservation on 20 January 2011. On the eve of its re-entry into service, on 2 April 2011, it took to the stage as star of a special evening photo shoot at the Didcot Railway Centre and looked splendid in its British Railways 'express' blue livery.

Locomotive portraits

The Keighley & Worth Valley Railway's Midland Railway 4F 0-6-0 No 43924 also has a special place in preservation history by being the first of more than 200 locomotives to be rescued from Woodham's scrapyard in South Wales. It arrived in Haworth in 1970 but due to the extensive restoration work required did not enter active service until 1974. Withdrawn again in 1987, the 4F returned to service following a major overhaul in 2011 and is here balanced on the turntable at Keighley station in March 2014. *Karl Heath*

BR Standard Class 8 4-6-2 No 71000 *Duke of Gloucester* was designed by R. A. Riddles at Derby in 1953 and constructed at Crewe Works in 1954. Only the prototype was constructed and the lack of consistency in its performances resulted in an operational period of just eight years. The locomotive had been earmarked to take its place in the National Collection, but for reasons unknown only one sectioned cylinder and set of valve gear were retained. The locomotive, like so many others, joined the scrap lines at Woodham's, Barry Island, until the 71000 Preservation Society was formed in 1973. That society has since undergone a number of changes itself, but over a period of 13 years the enthusiasts restored the locomotive to 'as built' condition. A number of modifications have now been made to the original design resulting in one of the most efficient steam locomotives ever to run in Britain.

Locomotive portraits

'To build and operate a Peppercorn Class A1 Pacific locomotive for main-line and preserved railway use' – this was the stated mission of the A1 Steam Locomotive Trust, and in August 2008 the first movement in steam of 'A1' Class 'Pacific' No 60163 *Tornado* was a major step towards that goal. The society has built a completely new 'A1' to the original design using the latest technology, and with an increased water capacity it is fully equipped to meet the challenges of operation on today's main line.

When outshopped it carried the Apple Green livery of the London & North Eastern Railway and was still carrying this when it visited the East Lancashire Railway in 2010.

Thankfully it is not only the 'glamorous' main-line express locomotives that have attracted the preservationists. There are plenty of smaller locomotives, many more than 100 years old, operating on our preserved lines. The London & North Western Railway Webb 'Coal Tank' is a prime example. This 0-6-2 tank locomotive was built at Crewe Works in 1888 and worked until withdrawal in 1958. After an initial period in private hands, its ownership was transferred to the National Trust, which put it on display at Penrhyn Castle in North Wales, a location not far from where it spent much of its working life. It was later put in the care of the Bahamas Locomotive Society at its then base at the Dinting Railway Centre near Glossop, where it was restored to working condition in 1980. In 1999 it was taken out of service for its third and most extensive overhaul in preservation, and this work was completed in 2011. When it visited the Severn Valley Railway in September 2012 it was carrying the livery from the period of ownership under the London Midland & Scottish Railway that followed the 'Grouping' of 1923. On the evening of 15 September 2012 No 7799 posed alongside the signal box at Hampton Loade.

Locomotive portraits

One of the oldest steam locomotives to be seen in active service in the world is the 0-6-0 well tank *Bellerophon*. It was built in 1874 by the Haydock Foundry to the design of one Josiah Evans, whose father Richard Evans owned the Haydock Collieries that would become Lancashire's largest privately owned mining concern. *Bellerophon* worked for 90 years right up to 1964, and in November 1966 the National Coal Board donated it to the Keighley & Worth Valley Railway. Ownership was later handed to the Vintage Carriages Trust, based at Ingrow on the railway, where it was restored. On 1 May 1985 it ran for the first time in preservation. *Bellerophon* is currently on loan to the Foxfield Railway, which provides an authentic industrial environment in which to see it.

Narrow gauge

The Ffestiniog Railway in Gwynedd, Wales, is the oldest independent railway in the world, having been founded by an Act of Parliament in 1832. It opened in 1836 and runs for just over 13 miles from the harbour at Porthmadog to the slate mining town of Blaenau Ffestiniog. Its purpose, when built, was to transport the slate from the mines down to the harbour where it was loaded onto ships. Up to the 1860s horse power was utilised to haul the empty slate wagons up to the mines. Once loaded the trucks would be assembled into trains and return to the harbour by gravity, controlled by brakemen. On special event days the railway recreates these gravity slate trains, and a journey in a slate wagon is a once in a lifetime experience (once is usually enough!).

In 1862 the railway sought tenders from manufacturers for is first steam locomotives. The following year a quotation received from George England & Co of Hatcham Iron Works, New Cross, South London, was accepted and it was not long before the first of the six locomotives built in South London arrived on the line.

On the evening of 2 May 2013 three of the railways 'England' locomotives were posed in front of the old shed at the line's Boston Lodge Works. Front left, in green, is *Welsh Pony*, the fifth locomotive built for the line in 1867. Front right is the second locomotive to arrive, in 1863, named *Princess* after Princess Alexandra of Denmark, who had married Albert Edward, Prince of Wales, earlier that year. To the rear is *Palmerston*, the fourth locomotive to be delivered, in March 1864. Viscount Palmerston was the Liberal Prime Minister and Chairman of the Welsh Slate Copper & Lead Mining Company's quarry at Blaenau Ffestiniog.

Narrow gauge

Narrow gauge

The Welshpool & Llanfair Railway in mid-Wales was opened in 1903 to serve the local industries along its route from the Oswestry & Newtown Railway's main-line station at Welshpool to the village of Llanfair Caereinion, a distance of 8½ miles. While most of the line has been preserved, the section that ran through the town of Welshpool to its station has not, and the preservationists have built a new terminus at Raven Square. However, the two original locomotives constructed for the line have remarkably been preserved and are maintained in working order to the delight of railway enthusiasts.

The first locomotive to arrive in 1902 was No 822 *The Earl*, with No 823 *Countess* arriving shortly after. Both had been built by Beyer Peacock & Company, Gorton, Manchester, and named in honour of the Earl and Countess of Powys in recognition of the support given by the Earl to the construction of the line.

When the railway was first opened it obtained three bogie carriages from R. Y. Pickering of Glasgow. These did not survive into preservation, being broken up in 1936, a few years after the cessation of passenger services on the line.

That would have been the end of the story, but the desire and perseverance of the society, supported by generous donors, has enabled a completely new rake to be constructed, to the original designs, by the Ffestiniog Railway at its Boston Lodge Works. The set was completed with the arrival of a third coach in August 2010.

Right: The gauge of the Welshpool line is 2ft 6in (762mm), which is unusual for British narrow-gauge railways and has meant that the society has had to look abroad for locomotives and stock to supplement the originals. One example is *Joan*, seen here by the coaling stage; built in 1929 by Kerr Stuart, it originally operated in Antigua.

Narrow gauge

Narrow gauge

The railway's annual gala sees all manner of steam vehicles in the yard at Llanfair, including showman's traction engines, and on the Saturday evening floodlights are set up to illuminate the scene, creating a multitude of photographic opportunities.

Steamy Nights

Narrow gauge

Over the weekend 12, 13 and 14 September 2014, after years of hard work and preparation by members, the Moseley Railway Trust staged a hugely successful 'Tracks to the Trenches' event to mark 100 years since the outbreak of the First World War and commemorate the role played by narrow-gauge railways in the conflict. The trust, based near Newcastle-under-Lyne in Staffordshire, operates the Apedale Narrow Gauge Railway and for this event had cleared and adapted a large area of land adjacent to its usual operations. These developments provided a narrow-gauge field railway complete with branches, a replica trench network and display area for cavalry. All of this was supplemented by a host of relevant visiting steam locomotives, a steam wagon, a traction engine, a replica tank and numerous Motor Rail petrol locomotives that trundled around the site all weekend.

On top of all this, to the delight of photographers a night shoot with cameos set up around the site was held on the Friday evening. A visitor from the Leighton Buzzard Light Railway was this Baldwin locomotive No 778, which dates from 1917. These were the most common steam locomotives operated by the War Department Light Railways during the Great War.

Later in the evening the Baldwin was lined up with the German military light railway's Henschel locomotive No 1091, a visitor from the Gloucestershire Warwickshire Railway based at Toddington. On the right is Kerr Stuart No 3014 of 1916, known as a 'Joffre' type (Marshal Joseph Jacques Cesare Joffre was the French Chief of Staff, responsible for the direction of the French war effort during the first two years of the Great War).

At the end of the evening attention turned to the replica 'ruin' where the Foden steam wagon and the recently restored Hudswell Clarke steam locomotive No 1238, built in 1916, were posed.

Narrow gauge

Left: A bonus for a night shoot at the Tanfield Railway was a local firework display in an adjacent field. *Karl Heath*

Middle left and left: For many years the Embsay & Bolton Abbey Steam Railway held a spectacular Bonfire and Firework Night, with the locomotive in service resting during the display.

Overleaf: This final photograph, taken by my son Karl, is of Williton station on the West Somerset Railway. With its preserved locomotive, trackwork, signalling and signal box, station building, platforms with their period fixtures, fittings and posters, it is a fine example of the railway preservation movement's ability to recreate the atmosphere of the working railway in the golden age of steam.